CULTURAL DIVERSITY IN THE WORKPLACE

Seeing Diversity Through Different Lenses

CULTURAL DIVERSITY IN THE WORKPLACE

Seeing Diversity Through Different Lenses

By

Dr. MaryAm Armani

BOOKSTAND
·PUBLISHING·
ESTD. 2006

www.bookstandpublishing.com

Published by
Bookstand Publishing
Pasadena, CA 91101
4980_3

Edited by Linda M. Weller

Cover Design by AD4U • A Design for You
(The image is procured from Adobe Stock)

ISBN 978-1-956785-78-4

DEDICATION

This study is dedicated to my parents for their unceasing encouragement, energy, and support, and for being my first coaches. My mother (TajMah Jon), a strong Persian woman, is my soul and has inspired me with her determination, dedication, courage, and profound philosophy of life. She has always supported my life decisions and guided me through the right paths of my journey. To my sharp, distinguished, and transparent father (Pedar Habib), who, with his free spirit, has taught and encouraged me to follow my curiosity and passion for different cultures. Since I left Great Persia (Iran) at a young age, I would get homesick and my parents would remind me of this poem by the great Persian poet, Rumi: "Wherever you stand, be the soul of that place!" My parents would comfort me and give me strength to overcome life's challenges. Who I am and where I stand today is because of them.

This dedication is also to the Persian (Iranian) young, energetic, intelligent, brave men and women who have not stopped fighting for their rights in the most perplexing and turbulent epoch of Persian (Iranian) history. Moreover, to three lands which have special places in my heart: Great Persia (Iran) my native land, which historically is well known as the Cradle of Culture, and a culturally passionate and enthusiastic nation; to Italy, my adopted land, a passionate country filled with deep historical culture and art; and to the United States of America, my second adopted land, a land of opportunity with a transparent and trustworthy society where I was taught to fly high and pursue my dreams, allowing me to put all of the missing pieces of the puzzle together in a way where I can achieve my goals.

PROLOGUE

I want to provide you with guidance and insights if you wish to work for a multicultural company, particularly one that serves cross-cultural populations. The challenges highlighted in my book revolve around navigating cross-cultural misunderstandings among a company's culture, customer service practices, and the diverse cultural norms and communication styles of the customer base.

I will also address American businesses in the United States that serve a variety of cultural populations, especially immigrant populations, as they often face misunderstandings about expectations on both sides. Misaligned expectations can lead to minor and major problems and disruptions. You will learn how to best understand and navigate the needs and expectations of other cultures within the context of customer service.

FOREWORD

Key aspects addressed in the book:

1. Understanding Cultural Diversity: Cultural diversity, including the various societal norms, values, and communication styles of different cultures.

2. Customer Service Across Cultures: Customer service practices vary significantly between cultures. This book explores these variations and their impact on interactions between companies and their diverse customer bases.

3. Communication Styles: Cultural communication styles, such as tone of voice, vocabulary, body language, time and space, and accent.

4. Cultural Competency and Inclusion: Cultural competency and inclusion in the workplace will be explained with helpful strategies for success.

5. Professional Identity Formation: Professional identity must be sensitively attuned to and inclusive of diverse cultural perspectives, thereby fostering a conducive workplace environment.

6. Intervention Strategies: Intervention strategies for effectively addressing cross-cultural challenges in customer service and other professional contexts.

This book is a valuable resource for those seeking to enhance their understanding of multicultural competency and improve their navigation of diverse cultural landscapes in the workplace.

I must emphasize that my book cannot and does not attempt to be exhaustive on the subject at hand, but is a rich culmination of numerous years filled with both adversity and triumph. My life journey has been characterized by a myriad of experiences, ranging from moments of profound joy to periods of profound challenge. These experiences, akin to a roller-coaster ride, have fundamentally shaped the individual that I am today. Indeed, my book is not merely an academic exercise, but a reflection of the depth and breadth of my personal growth. Each trial and tribulation have contributed to the development of my character and the formation of my identity.

INTRODUCTION

American businesses in the United States that serve multiple cultural populations, especially immigrant populations, face misunderstandings of expectations on both sides. Though some norms are easier to navigate, many are more subtle and can result in hurt feelings or even lost revenue when mishandled. Often, the damage is already done by the time the misunderstanding makes it to management.

Businesses dedicated to improving customer service can conduct sessions on cultural diversity awareness, customer service, and diverse cultural communication styles, such as tone of voice, vocabulary, body language, time and space, and accent. Appropriate teachers (contributors) would have personal experience in this area and work for an international company.

After many years of personal experience and listening to people's stories, it has become overwhelmingly obvious that cultural sensitivity and understanding within customer service is vital. Furthermore, employees' relationships, especially within highly diverse populations, must be nurtured and supported for long-term success.

TABLE OF CONTENTS

OVERVIEW OF MULTICULTURAL OPPORTUNITIES IN THE WORKPLACE

Multinational agencies in the United States that serve immigrants frequently contend with cultural misunderstandings. They can't be avoided. When people of different cultures communicate, they will necessarily misread words and or body language, thus necessitating the vital benefit of cultural sensitivity. It can be the difference between a successful transaction that leads to favorable outcomes or an outright disaster that can wreak havoc on a business or organization. In this book, I will discuss the gap between standard American customer service practices and the service preferred by most people from other cultures.

A government agency in California that serves a wide variety of populations has instituted a customer service orientation covering telephone conversations, accent, tone and volume of voice, vocabulary, and active listening. While well thought out and put together, this orientation failed to include an understanding of time from its curriculum. This omission impacts the customer in a variety of ways, such as in more frequent returns to the agency, lost work time, and missed deadlines due to insufficient information regarding necessary documents. The impact includes duplication, excessive customer interface (causing increased work hours), and inefficiency regarding the submission of needed documents. The result is often frustrated workers and customers, which can hurt the bottom line of any company. I wish to alleviate the misunderstandings that occur between customers and workers, no matter what kind of company is involved.

Working habits and hiring flows differ around the globe, but particularly between Eastern and Western cultures. For example, the Italian culture is complex and individuals tend to express their broad points of view at length. In the United States, communication is about cause and effect: the "why" and the "what." In still other cultures, communication is situational, which means people carry their common views into life's daily situations.

Despite the above examples, the different concepts of time have emerged as a frequent issue when serving immigrants. For instance, a 1-hour interview may seem more than sufficient to an American, but to an immigrant with multiple dilemmas, the same amount of time can feel inadequate, if not dismissive. The customer is looking for adequate time to socialize and understand cultural differences to avoid misunderstandings. Most workers in international settings, while familiar with a particular culture, are often unaware of the differences in communication styles within other cultures. This leaves a company vulnerable to minor and potentially major mishaps and lost opportunities. It is crucial for companies to properly train their customer service workers in the various communication styles of the cultures they work with most often. Only then can management trust that their customer service is going to help their bottom line instead of hurt it. All good business starts with relationship building.

Although technology can support customer service within international corporations, it cannot address cultural diversity among countries. Individual customers who enter U.S. agencies want to assimilate to their new land of opportunity and gain the most information possible with the least amount of misunderstanding and confusion. Newcomers to any country frequently experience culture shock and customer service providers can do a great service by ameliorating assimilation struggles, thus promoting quicker inclusion and integration into the new culture. Those from other cultures may also arrive with higher expectations of what customer service represents.

It's always good for a company when people of different cultural backgrounds (social, work, and education habits) adapt to each other in the workplace because racial diversity can also produce tension that can escalate into tension and anxiety that can hinder customer service. It can also damage the development and reputation of the organization itself. Conversely, if managed appropriately, a highly diverse environment can increase a business's value, such as through employee creativity, problem solving, and organizational potential. Also, to obtain an atmosphere of cooperation and success, upper management must genuinely appreciate the different backgrounds and cultures of its employees. Many laws, policies, and social/psychological ideas mean that employee status and upward mobility is impacted by race, gender, and ethnicity.

Understanding collectivism is vital to understanding the role of cultural diversity in the work environment. Cultures' rich values and customs are necessarily going to impact an organization's environment. NonU.S. managers can be perceptive to collectivism and respect that individuals and social relations frame groups. They believe in closeness among family members, which tends to create a high level of family obligation and loyalty, thus strengthening their sense of heritage. Companies also deal with issues such as change management, leadership and development, globalization, and diversity. Their job also involves establishing organizational and staffing structures, exploiting partnerships with local agencies, maintaining the company culture and legal integrity of the agency, and ensuring that it fits within the local culture. Therefore, it's beneficial to adapt the doctrines of systems-thinking in the

3

organization. Systems thinking explores a company system by analyzing operational methods, functionality, linkages, and interactions among departments and other components that make up the whole system. Systems-thinking relates to processes, linkages, and interconnections rather than structures, components, and separations. The focal point is the company's dynamic, which was created by a collaboration of systems that were implemented and combined by other systems. Once managers and leaders become system thinkers and comprehend the framework of their company's complexities, they can examine things from different angles. Discovering the rigid issues hindering an organization, while inherently challenging due to potential bias and interpersonal conflict, is an effective means to understanding the necessary frameworks of complex systems and schemes. Systems thinking is an essential part of successful leadership.

New technology can bring efficiency and convenience to the workplace, but the training it may involve can be stressful. It can also be hindered when long-term employees exhibit a *rusted mentality* stemming from a number of issues, such as general resistance to change, a stubborn preference for comfort zones and known routines, fear of the future, and unfamiliarity with the development plans and the transition process of the organization. A lack of familiarity with new technologies can also damage customer relationships when this dissonance runs up against expectations.

Stewart[1] illustrated the three phases of transition that facilitate the change process: The "letting go" phase, where one abandons previous experiences and old behaviors; (b) the "neutral zone," which encompasses moderately leaving behind old habits and prudently evaluating the future; and (c) the "new beginning," which happens when one mentally embraces the new change plan and completely accepts the new methodologies. The full transition period is a psychological process of accepting and working through the change. The list above seems logical and simple, and it is, but it's hardly easy. Let's delve a little further into this subject.

Long-term employees who resist the transition process tend to also fear the future. They question the desired outcome for the organization while struggling through the multiple stages of transition simultaneously. For this reason, thorough and thoughtful communication is vital. Managers must understand and accept the planned change concepts and the transition process and then ensure the message is delivered with clarity and trust so employees can build favorable attitudes toward the unknown. Open communication can best be achieved through active listening. Managers may want to offer meetings and training to introduce the planned changes at the micro level to facilitate slow, but full adjustment to each change in preparation for the next one. Every person carries their own abilities, perspectives, and expectations and it is the wise manager who works hard to help every employee work through this process individually and collectively for the best outcomes that will last and improve.

Cultural awareness in tasks impacts one's leadership style at every stage of the work cycle. When cultural diversity presents itself, whether environmental or educational, effective leaders look for and manage conflicts and misunderstandings with enhanced communication and understanding.

Although technology is vital for increasing and improving coaching methods, it's limited in interpretation when perceived from a cultural diversity context and is a perfect example of a technology misconception. Issues related to coaching have different meanings in each culture, leading to misunderstanding. For example, many cultures perceive time more slowly than do Americans; therefore, coaching approaches and learning must differ, especially with individuals who are unfamiliar with the complexities of cultural diversity.

Amy Cuddy's video, "Your body language shapes who you are"[2] connected with my experiences at certain points in my life and greatly motivated me. Her talk reinforced my viewpoint that communication occurs in different ways and sometimes there is no harmony between verbal and nonverbal communication. Also, as Cuddy stated, nonverbal behavior is another way of communicating and it can conjure judgments, sometimes with great subtlety. One facet of nonverbal communication is its ability to convey power in the absence of it. In other words, pretending to be a strong person can make you become a strong person! Dominant people are more confident and take more chances than do less confident people. Nonverbal expressions of power dominate the animal kingdom. Animals tend to expand their limbs and chests when they feel powerful in a moment of pride in the same way humans do, but when we feel fearful, we tend to hunch inward. All of these movements demonstrate the engagements of our body and mind, such as beliefs and feelings.

In this global marketplace, countless people travel and move frequently from one country to another for work, family, and educational reasons. Within this construct, it's vital that customer management provide additional skills for effective communication when delivering customer service in an international agency. Understanding cultural differences in communication helps international agencies provide competent and successful service to specific populations.

Something acceptable in one culture may not be acceptable in another, resulting in unintended offenses in the workplace that often clash with the organizational culture. A healthy company culture is vital to creating a safe and trustworthy work environment for employees' values regardless of race and background, as long as they fit within the company's culture, policies, and structures. Once an individual feels safe and valued intrinsically, he or she can be more positive, productive, and creative.

Furthermore, patience is important during the psychological development process, where the individual has not only needed to change his or her lifestyle naturally, but also needed to exchange current beliefs for unprejudiced notions. A person's approach to life and problem solving skills and how they operate among cultures (with regard to morals, values, structures, and regulations) is an interesting concept to explore. Cultural awareness is one of the most crucial factors in both working and living environments, especially in a multicultural country like the United States, where communication concerns frequently arise. Strong cultural backgrounds, approaches to life, problem-solving skills, personal lifestyles, and financial matters all contribute to enriching individual business and life goals.

I will now further explore cultural diversity, communication styles, customer service, and the use of language, time and space, tone of voice, accent, and body language.

OVERVIEW

Miscommunication can occur due to cross-cultural differences, even in the absence of problem attitudes. An example of this occurred at an opera I attended. The performers were Italian, South Korean, and Corsican. It was especially interesting to see how the artists communicated so easily through music with no concern for their differences. The South Korean singer performed the Italian opera songs beautifully, with only a slight accent. It would seem that applying similar diligence in the workplace could improve communication, as was so beautifully demonstrated in the music world.

CULTURAL DIVERSITY

Cultural diversity is not only about accepting people of different ethnic groups, but accepting their cultural differences as well. With regard to management techniques, it should be remembered that no one method works in all cultures. Also, if one can recognize and associate classes of culture that affect organizations, the value of the corporate culture will rise as well.

People who feel well regarded will generally be more positive and productive. Corporate culture is not only designed by technology and marketplaces, but by cultural differences that bring awareness of management and personnel. The importance of embracing cultural differences helps to explain one's own culture and how it affects others in the same environment. Inclusion is a fundamental approach to profiting from diversity that involves crafting and supporting working and living conditions. This allows and encourages individuality in the midst of differences and similarities within the workplace.

Managers who model and promote inclusive practices promote environments where employees feel valued and motivated to do their best work for the good of the team. Inclusion begins with acknowledging someone's personality and identity and allowing them to represent themselves as a complete individual. When we accept others' different interests and experiences, we can better appreciate the diversity all around and the accompanying perspectives. Each of us has a different familiarity with our own capabilities and talents and it is vitally important to engage with others in a cooperative and kind manner. While corporate culture policies can strain the work environment, sensible and fair organizational policies can promote esprit de corps and a willingness to contribute one's skills and talents. Furthermore, one must remember that beliefs, values, and personalities derive from social climates.

It is easily seen that self-inclusion can both decrease negative effects and increase positive ones for both the individual and the entire organization. Self-inclusion refers to the feeling of being accepted and valued within a group, organization, or society, even when cultural differences exist. While people often gravitate toward those who share similar backgrounds, languages, or customs, an inclusive organizational culture ensures that everyone feels welcomed and respected regardless of their differences. When diversity and inclusion are prioritized, individuals can contribute fully, leading to greater collaboration, innovation, and overall success. However, achieving this balance can also come with challenges, as diverse perspectives may sometimes lead to misunderstandings. Nonetheless, fostering a culture of inclusion is essential for promoting unity, harmony, and positive outcomes in any environment. People may want support from family members, friends, and society; but the type of support desired depends on personality and circumstances. Needs can pertain to emotions, education, or information. For example, a medical resident needs the support of family and friends during his or her arduous educational journey, especially if children are present. That same medical resident may need his coworkers to help him navigate the rigors of 30+ hour shifts. The ability of support to solve logistical problems or alleviate psychological stress differs from one situation to another and is determined by the type of support desired. All of these factors can bond individuals to the degree that communication, needs, and trustworthiness are present.

Beliefs and cultures exhibit variations in the promotion of individuals and ideas, which inherently influence their communication styles, particularly in the context of social movements. These differences stem from diverse cultural values, norms, historical contexts, and societal structures. As a result, cultures may embrace different approaches to communication within social activities.

In individualistic cultures, such as with the United States, autonomy is admired, which means that people value significance, appearance, principles, and personal success. People act independently, or appear to do so, and highly value freedom. By comparison, people behave more interdependently in collectivistic cultures, using their goals and thoughts for the greater good. These cultural differences dictate social support, the style of support used, and the means of seeking support.

While conducting research in upscale department stores, I observed that Asian American, Latino American, and African American employees in the sales department often assisted coworkers from the same cultural background during breaks or when help was needed. This behavior stood out because, despite working in the United States—an individualistic culture—these employees demonstrated a sense of collective support within their cultural groups.

They all worked harmoniously, embracing their cultural differences under the same organizational umbrella. Leadership and management had implemented policies and procedures that fostered a safe and inclusive environment, allowing everyone to collaborate effectively. As a result, employees were content because they consistently met their sales targets and the company benefited from increased sales. The researcher also occasionally noticed different cultural groups passing sales to one another, further highlighting the cooperative spirit in the workplace.

COMMUNICATION STYLE

A number of factors affect communication: body language, vocabulary, accent, tone of voice, culture, time, and space, making successful communication challenging for people of differing contexts. For example, Italians speak louder and more passionately than do Americans. Responses are generally "yes" or "no." The interpretation of these responses and tone of voice from people far outside of their contexts can cause misunderstandings. Cultural differences can be challenging in practice and style. The following areas of communication will further explain the dynamics of customer service and their differences.

CUSTOMER SERVICE – I

It's generally understood that customer satisfaction is determined by the quality of service and whether it meets one's needs. The customer's understanding and desires should always come first. Therefore, to succeed at customer satisfaction, a company dealing with a variety of cultures must necessarily acknowledge and include cultural diversity into its structure. This is especially significant with international customer service, where there is much more opportunity for misunderstanding and misinterpretation on both sides.

Customer service can vary significantly from one culture to another. If employees will not or cannot perceive a specific culture's point of view, huge misunderstandings, cultural turbulence, and possibly ruined company reputations can result. Too often satisfaction is viewed from only the customer's perspective, but it is also true that employee satisfaction directly correlates to customer happiness. In other words, content employees make for happier and more satisfied customers.

Within the greater marketplace, however, it is the customer service manager's job to represent the company's product or service. If the customer service center delivers a high quality product, and timely service, customers will be happy and loyal. It's also helpful to offer partial training programs to employees on products or services, customer service, communication abilities, and cultural aspects. Within the training, it's vital to teach cultural differences so that all customers can enjoy a pleasant buying experience, not just the ones native to the United States. With adequate knowledge and training, employees can better satisfy customers' needs, thus promoting loyalty and relationship.

Successful customer service within an individualistic culture, such as Germany's, is more about objectivity and competency. It is quite different from successful customer relations within a collectivist culture, like Portugal's, where customer relationships are primarily based on trust, even before it has been earned. Hence, a customer's personal style has to be respected at all times.

For example, in some East Asian cultures, like the Chinese culture, people are generally okay with waiting for their call to be answered, but they strongly dislike being put on hold. On the other hand, in cultures like Italian or Persian, people are generally fine with being on hold, if their calls are answered promptly when connected.

Honor significance is important in certain cultures, such as in the Middle East. If a male customer finds himself speaking to a female service representative, he will likely ask for a male or someone of comparable authority to himself. This request needs to be respected and acted on and should not be taken personally.

Relationships between customers and representatives are called "service encounters." Service encounters strongly shape customer satisfaction,[41] particularly when the communication is face-to-face. Frequently, consumers cannot choose their representative for a service encounter; therefore, consumers buying specific services may end up working with someone of a different cultural background called "service scripts," which is fundamental to reach client happiness and should be the company's goal.

The service script is a tool that allows customers to experience the representative's behavior throughout the service encounter and express their level of fulfillment with it. Service scripts can be one of the options that measures customer satisfaction in certain service areas. One especially important example is food service, where customer satisfaction is established in the quality of the service and the quality of the food, which is highly valued by most people.

Service scripts facilitate effective communication between service providers and consumers, particularly in situations involving individuals from different cultural backgrounds. By adhering to culturally sensitive scripts, service providers can navigate cultural barriers, misunderstandings, and conflicts, thereby fostering positive and productive interactions. Integrating culturally sensitive service scripts into customer interactions is instrumental to achieving client happiness, which should be the ultimate goal of any company. By recognizing and respecting cultural differences, companies can foster positive customer experiences, build trust and loyalty, and ultimately drive business success.

USE OF VOCABULARY/LANGUAGE VARIABLE

Many academics see language as a simple communication instrument and technique for exchanging ideas and thoughts. However, languages are quite complex, incorporating a series of lyrics linked by systems. Studying and mastering a foreign language, especially one of a much different style, like English versus Chinese, involves laboriously learning another culture's manner of exchanging of lyrics and systems in order to capture their essence of communication style. Language isn't simply an instrument of interaction, but a whole system of words, tones, body language and facial expressions. Language delivers numerous cues that direct our perceptions and understanding. In many ways it guides our very lives.

Additional concrete outcomes of nonverbal narrowness appear to occur throughout a dialog, mainly in the roundtable. The European American engages eye contact to remind them of rotation. The spokesman concludes the conversation by looking at the other person he is conversing with. If the spokesman looks down at the last moment of discourse, a set of babbles may start.

Contrary to this form, some Asian cultures generally avoid eye contact and pause among spokesmen. When speaking with people of cultures that embrace eye contact, Asians who are unfamiliar with norm might not get the chance to speak. Certain rituals of African American, Middle Eastern, and Mediterranean cultures select a "relay-race" form of roundtable. If an individual desires to be next, they just start speaking. Asian and European Americans are likely to perceive this habit as interference. The otherwise easy job of facilitating a meeting quickly intensifies in complexity when highly differing cultures are at play. The wise moderator will not ignore the differences, but seek to smooth over any that occur.

Men of European-American descent are generally straightforward and speak in a linear style, traveling from Point A to Point B, and so on, making contentions along the way, eventually arriving at a clear end. If somebody changes the direction of the conversation, he or she might say, "I'm not quite following you." or "Could we cut to the chase?" or "What's the bottom line?" In many institutions, this linear style has been recognized as a unique, symbolic, sharp, and analytical form of thinking. Nonetheless, it is not a traditionally common type of dialogue. A circular approach is preferred by Africans, as well as those in Latin, Arab, and Asian cultures.

Individuals who prefer a circular style have an ethnocentric explanation of the linear style and could look at it as equally naïve or egotistical: naïve due to the lack of complete elements essential to create a framework and egotistical due to the spokesman choosing which specific topics can be perceived and afterwards which topic can be drawn from. Moreover, promoters of a linear style tend to view the circular approach as unclear, ambiguous, and irrational.

Alternatively, variances in communication patterns are clear in conflict situations. Europeans and African Americans prefer straightforward speech when opposing someone's point, which contrasts with the circularity of Asians and Hispanics. A straightforward style, rather than a face-to-face argument of issues, and reasonably sharing emotions and an enthusiasm to say "yes" or "no" in response to demands is most effective in dealing with conflict. Individuals tied up in circular conversations look for third-party negotiators to lead tough debates, advise instead of state emotions, and defend people who offer what feels like vague responses to demands. An understanding of this fundamental difference among straightforward and circular styles is useful in accepting communication among Northern Europeans and U.S. Americans. Northern Europeans (especially Germans) lean toward candidness on logical subjects, but are reasonably indirect regarding social issues. For example, Northern Europeans are more likely than U.S. Americans to say, "That is the stupidest idea I've ever heard." Nevertheless, those same Northern Europeans are less likely than Americans to argue their emotions concerning people. U.S. Americans generally remain indirect on logical subjects, making remarks like, "Perhaps there's another way to think about that." or simply, "Hmmm, interesting." However, those same Americans believe that Northern Europeans are relatively arrogant, while Northern Europeans believe that Americans are superficial.

A high context (HC) interaction means that the bulk of evidence is presumed to be obvious in the person and very little is explicitly transferred in written form.[3] The opposite of this is low context (LC), where a great amount of information is transferred explicitly.[4] Japanese, Arabs, and Mediterranean populations who prefer strong information links with family, friends, coworkers, and customers are HC. In ordinary communications, they do not need or desire profound contextual information, as they are personally familiar with the goings-on of the most important people in their lives.

On the other hand, low-context individuals (Americans, Germans, the Swiss, Scandinavians, and other northern Europeans) compartmentalize their individual relations, jobs, and everyday lives.[5] Every moment that they must network with others involves specified contextual information. The French rank higher on the framework scale, requiring more contextual information than either the Germans or Americans. This difference can impact each circumstance and relationship unless these two opposing methods catch themselves.[74]

Folks in high-context cultures learn via their linkages, not wide-ranging contextual information.[6] In these societies, individuals do not count on language only for connection; tone of voice, timing, and facial expression are frequently used for sharing ideas. The authors of this research stated that the quantity of the reports is assigned explicitly in low-context societies. The Swiss compartmentalize their lives according to work and home. Consequently, when networking, they look for additional specific information. Societies vary in how their words communicate values and articulating all-inclusive, precise significance with correct word selection is essential. Moreover, in any kind of culture, battles can arise if expectations are not met according to cultural norms.

Native English speakers call others by their first names, which is inappropriate in the Persian culture, especially when youth are addressing adults. Also, the communicative tactic and regularity of greetings in Persian is essentially diverse from those who speak English.

Ethnic diversity also impacts whom should be admired. American or Australian women are comfortable speaking about their children's successes in school or group activities because they are only expressing pride in something well done. Conversely, this practice is considered rude in the Persian culture, as someone of proper modesty does not admire one's own family member in the presence of others.

Additionally, the idea of "Taarof" has a significant role in the Persian culture. It is a challenging perception that involves a broad spectrum of behavior and social status. "Taarof" is the principle insight of cultured graciousness in Persia, now known as Iran.

Researchers have investigated the differences in humor between Arabs and Americans using Hofstede's theoretical hypothesis about cultural dimensions.[7] The results showed that Americans scored significantly higher than did Arabs on self-enhancing and self-deprecating humor. Just as in general conversation, different styles of humor can be perceived adversely. In order to use humor as a positive communication, the motivator has to distinguish which humor types are adequate in the present circumstance.

There are four main humor styles: self-enhancing, affiliative, aggressive, and self-defeating.[8] Americans prefer self-defeating and self-enhancing humor. However, significant differences between Arabs and Americans do not exist in affiliative and aggressive humor. Arab males practice more aggressive humor than do females, and like the Arabs, American males practice more aggressive humor than do their female counterparts.

The Department of Labor's Secretary's Commission on Achieving the Necessary Skills report indicated that companies, on the communication talent scale, ranked security and retention of employment as highly important.[9] Companies also ranked verbal and written proficiency as extremely important and affirmed that communication skills had become fundamental to the workplace of the 21st century.[10] Effective communication results in professional achievement and improved income. Academy graduates rated communication classes as essential classes for their progress and development.[11]

High-tech firms in regions like the Silicon Valley (south of San Francisco) rated strong communication talents as equally important to technology skills. Companies believed that poor language proficiency decreased employability. "Many students come to me with poor English skills. I could not hire them because of our clients' perceptions."[12] Demand has increased for proficiency in public speaking, social talents, self-confidence, and enhanced cross-examining talents.

Companies now recognize the need for communication skills within the field of technology. However, they have struggled to acquire employees with sufficient writing and reading skills. Vocabulary and slang speech project as limitations, mainly among nonnative English speakers.[13] While the emphasis on good communication and language skills continues to increase and is sought after by companies, communication skills between English speaking and culturally diverse populations has had little emphasis in the U.S. culture or organizations.

TIME VARIABLE

The notion of time has been approached inversely in various cultures. In a practical community, time is money and it goes hand in glove with gaining or losing money. Time is valuable, so one must use it to make money, otherwise, one does not survive. In the American culture, lost time is lost income.

The concept of time is very diverse among Southern Europeans; consequently, they manage their time and lives differently from Americans. Southern Europeans prefer multitasking and pursue happiness and cheerfulness in their everyday lives. They do not commit to agendas or excessive obligations; hence, they see their lives as more meaningful than their meetings or plans, especially in countries like Spain, Italy, and Arabia. People are content to spend more time socializing, so long as people do not leave in the middle of a discussion. For instance, in Latin cultures, time is an occasion. It is discretely related and impossible to control. What the clock says doesn't matter.

In Mediterranean cultures, people highly value human connections and keep their relationships tight even during business meetings. They don't mind what time they meet or how long the meeting will take as long as they get their business completed; what matters is the meeting itself. In countries like America, or other linear-active countries, time is a chronometer (constantly ticking) connected to a timetable, or their agendas.

In multitasking countries, time is not carefully watched, but remains in the background. It matters, but rarely takes precedence over the occasion at hand. The Italians enjoy discussing their relatives, vacations, wishes, dramas, favorites, and more. Similarly, they are known for discussing their religion and political points of view. NonItalians should not feel awkward when conversing with Italians, as their seemingly shy or detached manner will not put off the more gregarious Italian. He or she will happily accommodate your shyness and foster an enjoyable encounter.

If you want to conduct business with Southern Europeans (Italian, French, Spanish, and Portuguese), you must realize that though they might seem willing to squander time, these people usually accomplish their meeting goals. The warm-up time served to get everyone on the same wave length and some of the "senseless digressions" led to creative solutions and agreements. He concluded that this optimistic courtesy of the Southern European culture is rarely duplicated in other cultures; instead, it is often criticized.

CULTURAL DIVERSITY IN THE WORKPLACE

For example, a Portuguese manager's supervisory approach, perceived as perpetually delayed, sets meetings with unreliable schedules. Likewise, the Portuguese manager's disfavored work scheduling doesn't appear to administer their time cost-effectively. They are distracted, arrive late, or fail to meet deadlines, even when they stay late in the evening—it's all for show. Mainly, in Southern-European cultures, work is focused on connections rather than timetables.

People within a Latin-based culture tend to take an individual approach, often called the "Latin Touch." It's an ability and connection that ultimately benefits the organization. In the Latin culture, people talk predominantly about relationships and social issues throughout their schedules, meaning that managers must keep people on task. However, when everyone ultimately desires the best for the company, it makes sense to allow flexibility while striving for moderation given today's fast and fluctuating markets.

Edward T. Hall, a pioneer in the study of time, proposed innovative categories of time.[14] The monochromic and polychromic times are very popular systems. Monochromic time is straight and simplistic and can be measured in consecutive ways, whereby it can be spared, kept, or lost. Monochromatic-oriented people in low-context cultures communicate clearly and openly, like in the U.S., or northwestern and central European countries.

Polychromic time is synchronized in real-time, which means that things happen simultaneously. Individuals will tackle numerous challenges with numerous people simultaneously, all the while considering the relationships and connections as most essential over meeting personal work deadlines. Polychromic, time-oriented people within high-context cultures live in Latin America, Asia, and the

Middle East. Individual family connections determine business ties and the amount of time given to interpersonal communication demonstrates the essential role of relationship over simple competency. People in monochromic time orientations focus more on finishing jobs.

Schuster and Copeland[15] presented the cultural time category system on a task-oriented and relationship-oriented scale and explained why traditional polychromic, time-oriented cultural groups are more concerned with long-term outcomes, versus their Western monochromic, time-oriented cultural groups. Monochromic people also engage in long-term projects, but they exist as straight and simplistic or discrete[16] and generally include early, mid, and distant goals or benchmarks. To the monochromic worker, tangible progress is the greatest form of success.

Based on the article, "Cross-Cultural Differences in Self-Reported Decision-Making Style and Confidence," decision making is a worldwide construct that runs into unique challenges when it involves individuals from different cultures.[17] Stewart[18] wrote about the main differences in the decision-making processes between Western and nonWestern people. He highlighted the contrast among the "technical" types of North America and the collective style of the Japanese. He also stated that "decision making for the Japanese is a social process first, not a cognitive and conceptual one, as it is with North Americans."[19]

Referring to "Cross-Cultural Differences in Self-Reported Decision-Making Style and Confidence," people in six countries were surveyed about decision making, with the variable being procrastination.[20] Participants were divided equally among Western (USA, Australia, and New Zealand) and nonWestern countries (Japan,

Hong Kong, and Taiwan). The scholars predicted that they would discover a differences in procrastination, expecting that since the East Asian students relied on group support, they would be more accepting of the decisions or consent resolutions of the group than would the Westerners. Additionally, there was a major differentiation between East Asian samples and Western samples. The scores of the Japanese and Taiwanese students (not Hong Kong) were higher on procrastination than for the Western students. The Japanese students had the highest scores in this survey. It was suggested that procrastination is possibly shown in group-oriented cultures when decision making is of mutual interest and individuals are expected to submit to the group and pause until the partners share their thoughts.

A stable and effective international trade demands resilient social and personal relations among individuals who are blended into diverse cultures.[21] Enhancing these types of networks depends on comprehending cultural likenesses and dissimilarities, which can have persuasive outcomes on how individuals interconnect with each other, come together for conclusions, and maintain agreements.

When it comes to time, people generally fall into two categories: flexible and inflexible. People who treat time with more flexibility are considered event driven and focus more on accomplishing their task than on timeliness. This is called being event driven and is frequently seen in in South America, South Asia, and economically developed countries where the fundamental focus toward clock time is not fully embraced.

On the other hand, people who look at time with more rigidity will begin to feel anxious or edgy when someone is running late or failing to complete something within a predicted amount of time.

These people tend to be clock watchers and will pay close attention to whether others are valuing their time and schedule.

Clock-based people also tend to arrange their days with different occasions and join in one event until it is over and then start another event. Clock time originated in North America, Western Europe, East Asia, Australia, and New Zealand.

Folks traveling internationally for trade should consider their multicultural proficiencies and avoid jumping to quick conclusions. Afterwards, they might want to analyze the situation for where they might have missed cues and could have been more respectful to the host culture. Ultimately, they should adjust their conduct in order to build more successful relationships.

The differences between clock-based and event-based time help explain the struggles of being on time. Within clock time, individuals feel obligated to show regret if they arrive late. Within event time, people may easily arrive at least 20 minutes late and not even apologize or otherwise comment.

People from certain countries will mention the rules of being on time by stating the meeting time. They do so by also including the name of the country. Where folks can attend the meeting at the later time, they often include words like "Filipino," or "Hawaiian" time. Timeliness is less of a stress in these situations. If the beginning time of the meeting is important, the name of the clock time culture is generally added, like "American" time.

In a nation like the United States, individuals dedicate the vast majority of their time to finishing their jobs and much less to socializing. In Latin American cultures, the approach is more 50/50. Americans often feel inefficient and noncompetitive in a fast moving world economy. Employees could initiate sympathetic job relations during these socializations, which may be called upon when a job has to be completed well and in a timely manner.

Social researchers, business travelers, and others can agree that various cultural clusters have diverse rules or routines when it comes to punctuality. Peace Corps helpers discovered that behind language barriers were extremely complex practices concerning the general pace of life and how punctual most people are[22]. Additionally, punctuality could be an ongoing problem in cross-cultural businesses.

Personal space can be described like an invisible structure that lets a listener know if he's getting too close or staying too far. Cultural diversity in private space now plays a greater role within socialization. In order to create and develop marketplaces worldwide and increase global collaboration, the issue of private space must be understood.

Hall's[23] four dimensions of private space (with Americans) can be used to establish the level of closeness within interactions and social activities. Intimate distance communicates a high level of closeness between two individuals. Personal distance is the interval between two individuals who know one another through close relations, like friends, brothers, or sisters. Social distance is about marginal and detached methods of interaction or professional affiliation; such as the relationships between colleagues, or in social entertainment. An individual tends to be mindful of his or her private space and reacts with a feeling of anger or discomfort when other individuals violate it

Private space is adjusted and modified according to culture. Private space is not only established through bodily distance, but through the emphasis of the presenters as well. Orientation is how an individual situates himself or herself beside another individual. Body position appears to be distinct even among ages and genders. German men tend to communicate more frankly than do American men. Italians, both female and male, were more straightforward than were Americans. However, American women dyads (couples) were more straightforward than were Germans, Italians, and other American (dyads) couples.

Considering social differentiations, Hall[24] studied diverse cultures and determined that personal space was minor among South Americans, Southern and Eastern Europeans, and Arabians. It is higher between Asians, Northern Europeans, and North Americans. Generally, cross-cultural research has indicated that people from North America and Northern Europe have greater areas of private space than do those from Mediterranean regions.[25]

In my own travels, when speaking to friends and colleagues who have traveled internationally, it has been widely seen that individuals in the United States, Canada, and England stand far apart, Europeans stand closer, and South Americans stand even closer. Scheflen and Ashcraft[26] found that the British, British Americans, and Black Americans stand nearly 36 inches apart in private conversations if space permits, whereas Mediterranean and Eastern Europeans stand closer together. Latin Americans tend to group jointly and within 24 inches of each other.[27] Navigating around these differences in space can prove confounding. For example, individuals in a group conversation might experience discomfort as the various members attempt to increase or decrease their personal spaces according to their individual preferences, creating additional awkwardness as the dance persists.

Hall[28] indicated that in the Middle East and Latin America, an American entrepreneur could be overwhelmed by issues regarding space. Folks might move very near to him, lay their hands on him, and generally crowd his personal space. When an American arrives in another country and acts contrary to the native norms, he is unintentionally offending, irritating, or fascinating the person with whom he or she is interacting or dealing.

In the United States, as compared to many other nations, males tend to prefer ample personal space when speaking. Systematic trade is shown at distances of around 5 to 8 feet.[29] Also, in the United States, it is entirely imaginable for a high-level manager to carefully plan the mediation phases; therefore, most employees feel calm knowing exactly what to expect. Trade deals grow in phases from stacks of paper on the desk to alongside the desk, to the coffee table, later to the meeting table, luncheon table, or the golf course, or, surprisingly, at the home, and all are related to the compound group of secret norms that are followed. However, in India and similar nations, it is inappropriate to discuss business inside a home or at social events. An individual in India would certainly not invite a professional associate to his house intending to debate trade deals. This would be an affront to acceptable hospitality.

Most, if not all, cultures have rigid and universal rules governing nonverbal interactions. In America and Europe, folks welcome everyone with a handshake and a smile. In East Asia, folks bow to one another with their hands at their sides, while in Thailand, folks bow with their hands in front of them as if in prayer. In the Middle East, folks bow with their hands on their hearts.

Cultures across the Mediterranean, Middle East, or Latin America communicate within smaller distances. Arab men are accustomed to very close seating, unlike their American counterparts. American men use more eye contact and talk in louder tones. Arabs have historically communicated in distances so close that they could feel the other individual's breathing.

Cultural diversity is learned in childhood and can be observed when children set up play dolls to socialize with one another. Beyond traditional customs, space utilized in social communications is also affected by the affiliation of the participants as well as their emotional tone.[30] As authors of this research reported, most evidence in regard to social space included dyadic or couples' communication. Limited evidence was found regarding use of space between groups of individuals, mainly foreigners throughout cultures.[31] Traditions also influence touch and how much is considered adequate. Care about preferred distances must be considered when interacting with persons of different cultures in order to avoid disruptions and offenses.

You might have also noticed that when people are speaking to someone who is using a less well-known language, the listener will tend to step a little closer to make sure they're hearing everything correctly, especially when discussing business. On the other hand, it may be debated that once communicating in another language, speakers can be seated at a distance because of unpleasantness. To test this, members of two different cultures were chosen to speak together twice, once in English and again in the other language. Based on the hypothesis, once these units communicated in English, one unit would accept a nearer distance and the other unit a further distance in contrast to when they communicated in their local languages. Supposing the legitimacy of the research, Japanese couples would sit closer to one another while communicating in English and Venezuelan couples would sit further away when communicating in English than when speaking in Spanish.

The subjects were 105 scholars at a big Midwestern university. Thirty-nine were American, 35 were bilingual Japanese, and 31 were bilingual Venezuelan. During enrollment, the subjects were told that the scientists were sociologists fascinated with dialogue. All subjects debated an identical theme. Twenty simple themes were examined with subjects from all three nations.

To obtain a significant sample, a same-sex, identical nationality ally assisted each subject of every group. Consequently, there were six associates: two Americans, two Japanese, and two Venezuelans; a man and a woman from each nation.[32] Associates were taught to perform in fairly identical ways. The scientist reminded them to consider matches and differentiations in a connection method and that they may be debating for an appointed theme (prefer games and interests) for 5 minutes. Foreign subjects later on learned that they were to communicate in whichever language they preferred.

Furthermore, it was expected that the Japanese participants would sit noticeably farther apart than would the Venezuelans, with the Americans being seated in the middle. Afterwards, it was noticed that the Japanese were seated farther away than were the Venezuelans and the Americans, though the Americans and Venezuelans did not vary drastically. Additionally, the observers noticed that while communicating in English, Venezuelan subjects sat further away than when communicating in Spanish, and Japanese subjects sat closer together when communicating in Japanese.

ACCENT VARIABLE

In dialogue, there is always a speaker and at least one listener. When miscommunication occurs, whose fault is it? Of course, people differ on this point. In business communication, especially between people of different languages and cultures, finding who's to blame is much less important than figuring out what went wrong and how to correct it. Both sides always bear a certain amount of responsibility and successful communicators will respectfully seek clarification even when they feel less at fault or that someone's accent is exceedingly difficult to understand.

It should be further noted that one should take special care to not ridicule or criticize someone for their accent because it is surely not something they can control very easily. A polite and respectful request that the person repeat themselves is all it should take to gain understanding and then proceed with the conversation at hand. In doing so, you will avoid making the other person feel insulted rather than simply a mutual participant facing normal language barriers. Be sure that members of certain cultures, especially in America, are sensitive to bias and can be easily hindered if they perceive that you are juding their accent as a character quality instead of a natural indicator of their original language.

Peter Ball[33] led a number of tests on central European accents. Research on high school learners from Italy, France, Germany, and Australia received Pronunciation English forms. The outcomes showed that for English, the shape of articulation is a time-consuming observation that happens typically with British accents. Also, in other European accent research, French and German-sounding speakers were perceived as more intelligent, while German-sounding people were thought to be more expert. Once a listener interacts with a presenter who has a dialect or different pronunciation from them, the listener can change to the new language quickly even though the listener initially struggled to understand the presenter. Soon, listeners can comprehend different pronunciations and better recognize what the presenter is saying. This practice is moderately common and instinctive. People who criticize others' accents are, intentionally or not, putting responsibility for successful speech on the presenter rather than accepting equal obligation as the listener to help ensure successful communication. Widely available data show that just 5% of the global population will be innate English speakers by 2050, which is less than 7% of the world's population.[34]

Accents represent distinct methods of delivering speech. Certainly, each person has an accent, and no accent, innate or not, is naturally better. Esling and Wong[35] argued that lifelong formations of the vocal tract differ according to language. Transmitting these formations from an L1 [primary language] into an L2 [secondary language] is a significant foundation of accentedness. We recognize accentedness in the way that diverse forms of dialect echoes contrast to the native selection. Certain accents, especially European ones, are linked to style as a result of several people having purposely accepted nonnative language forms, such as Leopold Stokowski, the well-known artist. He was born and raised in London, England, but spent his entire life traveling between the United Kingdom and the United States. Even so, in broadcasting conversations, he usually communicated with a distinctly Eastern European accent. Maurice Chevalier was apparently contractually required to emphasize his French accent with his movie studio on account of fans who preferred his charming voice.

Although accents have benefits, they have deficits too. Efficiency in clearness is the best evidence. Misunderstandings can occur even when grammar and terminology are understood and this can be stressful or uncomfortable for both the presenter and listeners. The most important feature of language is that it limits the capacity to modify one's language forms. Without ignoring finer features of accent, the point is that numerous second language presenters face judgment in response to their accented dialects.

Furthermore, a strong link exists between accent and race. Munro[36] recognized three kinds of accent judgments. First is *stereotyping*, usually across boundaries. Individuals who dislike Iraqis, for example, might hear a Middle Eastern accent on the telephone and refuse to provide service to that person. The second kind is *harassment*. For instance, a colleague might imitate the second language accent in a mocking tone. The third kind of judgment, *discrimination*, happens once a potential worker is told that his or her accent is undesirable for a certain job despite the occupation not demanding linguistic proficiencies. The emphasis is on accents, but that is not the real reason; it is the frequent narrow-mindedness of unilingual speakers. Listeners can be disappointed with even the purest second language presenter only because he or she has decided that accented discourse will be difficult to comprehend.

While migration is growing internationally, public reactions to migrants and migration everywhere has been generally unaccepting. Even undesirable manners are pointed out to tourists. A foreign accent is the most noticeable feature of individuals from other nations who move to live, work, or study in new countries, making them easy targets. It is a reminder that the individual is not a local and, additionally, that the individual lacks linguistic proficiency regardless of intelligence.

Furthermore, linguistic deficiency has several unpleasant consequences, varying from the psychological to the economic. An accent expresses one's manner of pronunciation, forms a significant portion of the presenter's public character, and provides a broad amount of public information. Also, innate accents develop in children as young as 5 months,[37] suggesting that accents are influential organizational signs, nevertheless, of public references. Therefore, people who are confident in a second language usually communicate with a noninnate accent, despite several years in the host state.[38] Nealry all of us have seen how Disney films excessively exploit nonnative accents in undesirable or clichéd ways. This is a subtle form of discrimination that can lead to a lifetime of bias.

Standard accents in a particular state are often accents of the cultured high classes and are viewed as more attractive, respected, and enjoyable to hear than are nonstandard, lower class, or traditional accents.[39] reported that Innate English-speaking nations, such as England, Australia, and those in Western Europe are admired,[40] whereas accents of other nations are usually considered less impressive.[41] However, it's been my experience that listeners don't need to perfectly distinguish someone's accent in order to make judgements and generalizations.

In the United States, Title VII of the Civil Rights Act of 1964 "forbids bias based on national origin;" however, it does not specifically indicate accents.[42] Based on Derwing and Research has shown that applicants' accents were modified due to both circumstances and mindful determination.[43] Sixty percent of applicants reported that they were able to change their accents by concentrating on certain portions of a phrase. So, 60% indicated that their accents changed once they were anxious or enthusiastic.[44]

Another researcher argued that a presenter's pronunciation or dialect could provoke optimistic or undesirable perceptions in the listener.[45] Accent has been described as a distinctive kind of sound invention made with a presenter's tongue or local language. Even though change in semantics is a main element of accents, prosody, involving rhythmic stress and emphasis, also contributes.[46] Overall, pronunciation can be understood as a person's territorial basis, local linguistics, or public position. Once English is communicated as a second language, the dialectic features of the primary or innate language can be transferred into English, developing an accented English.[47]

Other research examined the impact of pronunciation on prospective employees throughout an interview for a Human Resources Director position.[48] Applicants from the United States were required to assess a participant with accents from the Midwestern part of the United States, France, and Colombia, hearing through acoustic profiles. The outcomes demonstrated that the participant with the Midwestern pronunciation was assessed more positively than were the other participants. This outcome proved that people are drawn the others who sound like themselves. It isn't so much about several people having an accent while other people do not as much as it's about finding similar-sounding language most pleasant and easy to hear.

Another example is that Mexican American presenters with heavy accents generally obtained lower-level jobs than did those with lighter accents.[49] Also, among managerial positions, individuals using typical American English enjoyed better hiring success than individuals with African American English accents, Spanish-affected English, or Southern White English.[50]

TONE OF VOICE VARIABLE

Americans who communicate with Asians, such as the Japanese and Filipinos, are usually confounded because their Asian counterparts do not always reply in kind once they say "yes," like

Americans do.[51] On the other hand, many Asians get confused by their American friends because they usually do not "get it." Underlying this occasional mishap in international connections is an ethnic difference in instinctive attentiveness to various features of expressions.[52] Where Americans focus mainly on vocal content, Asians listen carefully to the oral tone and related words. Furthermore, in most Western cultures, much more significance and meaning is given to oral content.

During social networking, voiced emotional expressions, as well as facial expressions, confirm persuasive connections. Facial expressions are known as the worldwide language of sensation, but some have proved that multicultural differentiations in facial expression within Western and Eastern clusters remain.[53]

In each civilization and language, people enthusiastically sound out certain words to make big but simple statements.[54] For example, think of the word "Good!" When this generally positive word is spoken in a tough or harsh vocal tone, the listener will probably assume that the speaker doesn't mean it in a favorable way. A methodical study by Scherer[55] collected extensive examples of how voice expression is precisely distinguished on a minor, uncultured level of niceness and provocation. Moreover, many researchers, guided predominately by English presenters, have started to recommend various techniques in which vocal content (what is said) and tone of voice (how it is said) together manage communication[56] and public opinion.

Here's a great example: In January, 1991, The New York Times broadcasted a conference that hosted the Foreign Minister of Iraq, Tariq Aziz, and the United States Secretary of State, James Baker. A miscommunication occurred regarding James Baker's well-defined statement that the United States would attack Iraq if they did not liberate Kuwait. However, he expressed it with a gentle tone. The misperception occurred because Saddam Hussein's brother observed only Baker's demeanor and tone of voice rather than the content as well. He informed people in Baghdad that "the Americans will not attack. They are weak. They are calm. They are not angry. They are only talking."[57] We already know that Western cultures emphasize content over nonverbal cues. Therefore, it's not surprise that Hussein's brother, who was not familiar with Western culture, misinterpreted Baker's message.

On the other hand, Baker did not direct his speech to Aziz. It was uncertain if Baker was speaking to someone specific. Individuals cannot modify their demeanor that radically only because they are networking with people of other societies. It isn't clear what Aziz described to Hussein; however, it's possible that Hussein took special consideration into his brother's evaluation, since trust in collectivist cultures gives more value to those within its boundaries than outside of them. Nevertheless, the war commenced following that gathering. Cultural diversity frequently leads to misperceptions and battles. Battles are bigger between cultures that are drastically diverse versus ones that are alike. This is known formally as "cultural distance."[58]

Regarding nonverbal communication, vocal expressions are essential to highly expressive people because of differences in tone, strength, rhythm, and silences.[59] These variations in voiced qualities relate to transformations in breathing, pronunciation, and speech. This can be seen with Italians, for example. In a work environment, Italian applicants are expected to be orally more expressive given their stereotypically demonstrative and passionate Latin Mediterranean culture. Chinese applicants, on the other hand, have a thicker dialogue level and slower breaks in the oral expression of emotion. In respect to voice tone signals in communicating emotions, Chinese applicants changed less from their soft voice than did the Italian applicants. All of these observations can be very useful in the work setting, particularly in customer work, where people can make quick impressions about a company based solely on perceptions and feelings.

CROSS-CULTURAL DIVERSITY

The theme of miscommunication gets magnified because of cross-cultural environments and miscommunication can be based on one's mindset or perception. For example, asking "How are you feeling?" can be perceived as friendly, judgmental, or neutral. It can be difficult to accept communication if it's perceived as negative. A negative or positive perception can take the receiver to an emotional state. Additionally, if the original communicator isn't aware of their misunderstanding that just took place, he or she is prone to think the listener is being rude or difficult. This can lead to more misunderstanding that can eventually lead to complete relational breakdown.

Many of us derive support from our families and friends; however, the type of support depends on the personality of the individual and the circumstances in which he or she finds himself. The nature of the support can be emotional, educational, or informational, and all are subject to the kind of support a person is seeking. For example, a politician needs the support of family and friends for his or her campaign. On another occasion, he or she may need their coworkers' support for time management at work. The values of support, both for solving the problem and psychological stress, can differ from one situation to another and is determined by the type of support desired. All of these factors create closeness among individuals. Furthermore, the degree of closeness can vary depending on the context of communication, needs, and trustworthiness.

Perceiving the importance of cultural differences helps us understand how our own cultures affect other people in social settings. When we accept that people's interests and experiences vary widely, we can see the surrounding diversity through a different lens. Every person has a different familiarity with his or her own background, behaviors, capabilities, and talents and it's beneficial to engage with and fit these all together.

Corporate culture, beyond the individual, is not only designated by advanced technology, the environment, and marketplaces, but also by cultural differences in policies and procedures. It is daunting to comprehend and takes great effort to work with corporate culture policy; however, organizational policy can put employees at ease, allowing them to fully utilize their skills and experiences.

COMMUNICATION STYLES

Cultural differences are challenging in practice and style. Communication involves body language, vocabulary, time and space differences, tone of voice, and understanding differences in accent. All of these work together to effectively or ineffectively deliver the intended message to the customer from the employee, or vice versa. The successful communicator will customize his or her use of the various methods for the benefit of his or her present audience.

Communication can be challenging and is frequently incorrectly executed. For example, Italians speak more loudly and passionately than do Americans, and their responses are generally "yes" or "no." Americans often misinterpret these responses and tones of voice without realizing it. Customer service representatives must avoid misunderstanding in communication with their clients in order to successfully provide services.

CUSTOMER SERVICE – II

Customer service naturally varies from one culture to another. Conducting customer care improperly can cause simple misunderstandings, cultural turbulence, and possibly a ruined company reputation. Employee satisfaction and customer happiness correlate; however, it's the customer service manager's main responsibility to represent the company's product or service in the marketplace. If the customer service center delivers a high quality and worthwhile product and timely service, the customer will be happy and remain loyal.

Successful customer relations see the individual within the group. The employee who knows that the individualistic German culture values objectivity, competency, structure, and technical abilities will adjust their approach to highlight these qualities. The relationship is very different in a collectivism culture, like Portugal's, where trust preempts all business relationships, even between that of a customer and service representative. However, whether individualistic or collectivistic, the customer's privacy must be respected at all times.

In some East Asian cultures, people generally accept waiting for their call to be answered, but they strongly dislike being put on hold . Moreover, the *honor significance* is very important in certain cultures, such as those in the Middle East. If the customer service representative is a young woman, the male customer will instead want to speak with a person he considers at his same level or authority. The request to be transferred should be respected and the representative should not be offended by the request. Quality customer service will depend on the ability to meet the customer's expectations with respect and understanding.

The impact of cross-cultural understanding and the ability to interact with others in the world is critical to the image and reputation of an organization. Often the conflict that arises between different cultures is due to avoidable misunderstanding and not appreciating cross-cultural differences.

While cross-cultural awareness is important to quality customer care in the United States, it is also important to international companies that have diverse employee and client populations. The need for expanded thinking about how to interact in a global economy is increasingly crucial in today's business world. Companies actively working in the international climate must accept that countries possess different ways of approaching issues and training regarding motivating and evaluating their employees. It's vital for employees and company leaders to consider and understand the policies and procedures of the country of interest and learn how to effectively work within those differences.

The need for cross-cultural awareness and understanding is a broad concept that applies to both macro and micro systems, such as countries, organizations, individuals, politics, work environments, communities, and personal relationships. At the micro level, I hope to enhance customer service in the cross-cultural setting. As individuals, our life stream is affected by constant change. In organizations, where change is also constant, interventions may be recommended based on the challenging issues they face, which can be related to environment or company culture; such as customer service relationships, communication, decision-making, leadership styles, policies, procedures, and customer, employee, or service satisfaction. A healthy relationship with a client means balancing the values and cultures of both the customers and the organization and how its employees project their culture.

Many years of experience in sales, marketing, and customer service throughout different economic, political, and religious climates taught me that success is made greater with the help of a sharp mentor and coach who teaches how to better shape, structure, and bring together all of the implicit and explicit knowledge. I truly hope that reading and studying my book made you feel valued and mentored and that you will go on to find new successes in your personal and business endeavors.

ENDNOTES

1 Stewart, K. A. (1992). Managing transitions: Making the most of change. *Human Resource Planning, 15*(3), 93-95.

2 Cuddy, A. (n.d.). *Your body language may shape who you are.* https://www.ted.com/talks/amy_cuddy_your_body_language_sh apes_who_you_are?langauge=en.

3 Hall, E. T. (1989). *Beyond culture.* Anchor.

4 Bennett, M. J. (1998). Intercultural communication: A current perspective. Basic concepts of intercultural communication: Selected readings (pp. 1-34). Intercultural Press.

5 Treven, S., Mulej, M., & Lynn, M. (2008). The impact of culture on organizational behavior. *Journal of Contemporary Management Issues, 13*(2) (Special issue), 27-39.

6 Ibid.

7 Kalliny, M., Cruthirds, K. W., & Minor, M. S. (2006). Differences between American, Egyptian and Lebanese humor styles: Implications for international management. *International Journal of Cross Cultural Management, 6*(1), 121-134.

8 Martin, R. A., Puhlik-Doris, P., Larsen, G., Gray, J., & Weir, K. (2003). Individual differences in uses of humor and their relation to psychological well-being: Development of the Humor Styles Questionnaire. *Journal of Research in Personality, 37*(1), 48-75.

9 Stevens, B. (2005). What communication skills do employers want? Silicon Valley recruiters respond. *Journal of Employment Counseling, 42*(1), 2-9.

10 Locker, K. O., & Kaczmarek, S. K. (2001). *Business communication: Building critical skills.* McGraw Hill-Irwin.

11 Stevens, What communication skills do employers want?

12 Ibid.

13 Ibid.

14 Brodowsky, G. H., Anderson, B. B., Schuster, C. P., Meilich, O., & Venkatesan, M. V (2008). If time is money is it a common currency? Time in Anglo, Asian, and Latin cultures. *Journal of Global Marketing, 21*(4), 245-257. 10.1080/08911760802206003.

[15] Schuster, C. P., & Copeland, M. J. (1996). *Global business: Planning for sales and negotiations*. The Dryden Press.

[16] Graham, J. L. (1981, Fall). A hidden cause of America's trade deficit with Japan. *Columbia Journal of World Business, 16*, 5-15.

[17] Mann, L., Radford, M., Burnett, P., Ford, S., Bond, M., Leung, K., & ... Yang, K. (1998). Cross-cultural differences in self-reported decision-making style and confidence. *International Journal of Psychology, 33*(5), 325-335. 10.1080/002075998400213.

[18] Stewart, E. E. (1985). Culture and decision making. In W. B. Gudykunst, L. P. Stewart, & S. Ting-Toomey (Eds.), *Communication, cultural, and organizational processes*. Sage.

[19] Ibid.

[20] Ibid.

[21] Brislin, R. W., & Kim, E. S. (2003). Cultural diversity in people's understanding and uses of time. *Applied Psychology: An International Review, 52*(3), 363-382. 10.1111/1464-0597.00140.

[22] Spradley, J. P., & Phillips, M. (1972). Culture and stress: A quantitative analysis. *American Anthropologist, 74*(3), 518-529.

[23] Hall, E. T. (1959). *The silent language*. Anchor.

[24] Hall, E. T. (1966). *The hidden dimension*. Doubleday.

[25] Beaulieu, C. J. (2004). Intercultural study of personal space: A case study. *Journal of Applied Social Psychology, 34*(4), 794-805. 10.1111/j.1559-1816. 2004.tb02571.x.

[26] Scheflen, A. E., & Ashcraft, N. (1976). *Human territories: How we behave in space-time*. Prentice-Hall.

[27] Beaulieu, Intercultural study of personal space: A case study.

[28] Hall, E. T. (1960). The silent language in overseas business. *Harvard Business Review, 38*(3), 87-96.

[29] Ibid.

[30] Little, K. B. (1968). Cultural variations in social schemata. *Journal of Personality and Social Psychology, 10*(1), 1-7. http://dx.doi.org/10.1037/ h0026381.

[31] Matsumoto, D., & Hwang, H. C. (2016). The cultural bases of nonverbal communication. In D. Matsumoto, H. C. Hwang, M. G. Frank, D. Matsumoto, H. C. Hwang, & M. G. Frank (Eds.), *APA*

handbook of nonverbal communication (pp. 77-101). American Psychological Association. 10.1037/14669-004.

[32] Forston, R. F., & Larson, C. U. (1968). The dynamics of space: An experimental study in proxemic behavior among Latin Americans and North Americans. *Journal of Communication, 18*, 109-116. http://dx.doi. org/10.1111/j.1460-2466. 1968.tb00061.x.

[33] Ball, P. (1983). Stereotypes of Anglo-Saxon and non-Anglo-Saxon accents: Some exploratory Australian studies with the matched guise technique. *Language Sciences, 5*(2), 163-183.

[34] Eisenchlas, S. A., & Tsurutani, C. (2011). You sound attractive! Perceptions of accented English in a multilingual environment. *Australian Review of Applied Linguistics, 34*(2), 216-236.

[35] Esling, J., & Wong, R. (1983). Voice quality settings and the teaching of pronunciation. *TESOL Quarterly, 17*, 89-94.

[36] Munro, M. J. (2003). A primer on accent discrimination in the Canadian context. *TESL Canada Journal, 20*(2), 38-51.

[37] Kinzler, K. D., Dupoux, E., & Spelke, E. S. (2007). The native language of social cognition. *Proceedings of the National Academy of Sciences of the United States of America, 104*(30), 12577-12580.

[38] Munro, M. J., & Derwing, T. M. (1995). Processing time, accent, and comprehensibility in the perception of native and foreign-accented speech. *Language and Speech, 38*(3), 289-306.

[39] Cargile, A. C., Giles, H., Ryan, E. B., & Bradac, J. J. (1994). Language attitudes as a social process: A conceptual model and new directions. *Language and Communication, 14*(3), 211-236. P. 217.

[40] Lippi-Green, R. (1994). Accent, standard language ideology, and discriminatory pretext in the courts. *Language in Society, 23*(2), 163-198.

[41] Lindemann, S. (2005). Who speaks "broken English"? U.S. undergraduates' perception of nonnative English. *International Journal of Applied Linguistics, 15*(2), 187-212.

[42] Gluszek, A., & Dovidio, J. F. (2010). The way they speak: A social psychological perspective on the stigma of nonnative accents in communication. *Personality and Social Psychology Review, 14*(2), 214-237.

[43] Derwing, T. M., & Rossiter, M. J. (2002). ESL learners' perceptions of their pronunciation needs and strategies. *System, 30,* 155-166.

[44] Gluszek, The way they speak: A social psychological perspective on the stigma of nonnative accents in communication.

[45] Edwards, H. T. (1997). *Applied phonetics: The sounds of American English* (2nd ed.). Singular.

[46] Lippi-Green, R. (1997). *English with accents: Language, ideology, and discrimination in the United States.* Routledge.

[47] Carlson, H. K., & McHenry, M. A. (2006). Effect of accent and dialect on employability. *Journal of Employment Counseling, 43*(2), 70-83.

[48] Deprez-Sims, A. S., & Morris, S. B. (2010). Accents in the workplace: Their effects during a job interview. International *Journal of Psychology, 45*(6), 417-426.

[49] Brennan, E., & Brennan, J. (1981). Accent scaling and language attitudes: Reactions to Mexican American English speech. *Language and Speech, 24*(3), 207-221.

[50] Deprez-Sims, Accents in the workplace: Their effects during a job interview.

[51] Barnlund, D.C. (1989). *Communicative styles of Japanese and Americans: Images and realities.* Wadsworth.

[52] Ishii, K., Reyes, J. A., & Kitayama, S. (2003). Spontaneous attention to word content versus emotional tone: Differences among three cultures. *Psychological Science, 14*(1), 39-46. 10.1111/1467-9280.01416.

[53] Jack, R. E., Garrod, O. G., Yu, H., Caldara, R., & Schyns, P. G. (2012). Facial expressions of emotion are not culturally universal. *Proceedings of the National Academy of Sciences of the United States of America, 109*(19), 7241-7244.

[54] Kitayama, S., & Ishii, K. (2002). Word and voice: Spontaneous attention to emotional utterances in two languages. *Cognition and Emotion, 16*(1), 29-59. 10.1080/0269993943000121.

[55] Scherer, K. R. (1986). Vocal affect expression: A review and a model for future research. *Psychological Bulletin, 99*(2), 143-165.

[56] Kitayama, S. (1996). Remembrance of emotional speech: Improvement and impairment of incidental verbal memory by

emotional voice. *Journal of Experimental Social Psychology, 32,* 289-308.

[57] Triandis, H. C. (2C00). Culture and conflict. *International Journal of Psychology, 35*(2), 145-152. 10.1080/002075900399448 p. 145.

[58] Ibid.

[59] Juslin, P. N., & Laukka, P. (2003). Communication of emotions in vocal expression and music performance: Different channels, same code? *Psychological Bulletin, 129*(5), 770.